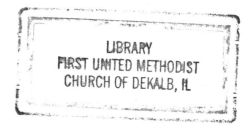

beginning

PRAYER

10
RIL

beginning
PRAYER

JOHN
KILLINGER

UPPER
ROOM BOOKS®
NASHVILLE

Cover and interior design: Bruce Gore / www.gorestudio.com

Library of Congress Cataloging-in-Publication Data
Killinger, John.
  Beginning prayer / John Killinger.
    p. cm.
  ISBN 978-0-8358-1186-6 (print)—ISBN 978-0-8358-1187-3 (mobi)—
  ISBN 978-0-8358-1188-0 (epub)
  1. Prayer—Christianity. I. Title.
  BV215.K47 2013
  248.3'2—dc23
                        2012035612

Printed in the United States of America

With love and best wishes to
BILL AND AUDREY COWLEY,
whose prayers have often been a welcome gift in my life.

CONTENTS

INTRODUCTION

If there is one sin that hurts us more than all others, it is surely the sin of not praying. We are meant to live in the Spirit of God—to live joyously, vibrantly, and lovingly in the world. But if we do not pray, we cannot live in the Spirit. It is as simple as that. We lack the daily connection to God that would make such a wonderful life possible.

How many resources for happiness and power we squander this way. How many of us never reach the fulfillment intended for us. How much frustration and sorrow we endure all because we do not really know how to pray and live in the Spirit.

And how much poorer the world is because of it!

This is not because we do not believe in prayer. We do believe in it. If a poll were taken of all the Christians in the world, it would show an astonishingly high percentage of belief in the power and efficacy of prayer. The world has changed greatly in the last few years, but nothing has happened to eradicate our faith in prayer.

The problem is that we simply do not know *how* to pray. Many of us do not know the first thing about praying. We do not even know how to begin. We are like babies who are given lectures on the glory of walking, and shown movies about the places to which we can walk once we are ambulatory, when what we really need is someone to take us by the hand and help us to put one foot in front of the other.

There are many wonderful books about prayer. Some describe the bliss of the experience of prayer. Others deal with the psychological benefits to the person who prays. Still others treat the more difficult question of intercessory prayer, and how our prayers are helpful and supportive to those for whom we pray.

But those are books for the person who already knows how to pray, who has had at least an introduction to the actual experience of prayer and merely needs encouragement to keep at it or some word about refining his or her technique.

This book is different. This book provides a very basic introduction to what one does when he or she begins to pray. It assumes that the person reading it knows very little about the experience of prayer; that he or she really wants to learn how to pray; and that he or she is ready to take the first fumbling steps and get the feel of what prayer is all about.

This is simply a book of suggestions about where to begin.

About *attitude* in prayer.

About *times of the day* for praying.

About *the best place* for prayer.

About *posture*.

About *mood*.

And then, most importantly, about *specific methods* for beginning to pray.

Some of the methods may be ones you have tried before. In that case, you may wish to skip them and go on to the other methods.

The point is, this is a book about mechanics. It is a simple how-to book, a book written for the novice and real beginner. It assumes no experience at all on the part of the reader. Its accent is on very basic and practical matters.

If you are already beyond this stage and are looking for something more inspirational, then you would do well to look elsewhere. Here we shall be dealing with fundamentals.

AN ATTITUDE OF PRAYER

WHAT DO YOU expect from prayer? Your attitude can make a great difference in the degree of success you encounter.

As people who know best will tell you, the benefits of prayer rarely come in terms of what you expect when you begin to pray. In that way, prayer is like marriage. Its greatest fruits are unimaginable at the stage where one stands before the altar; they come slowly, sometimes imperceptibly, through the years. Even then they are seen most clearly in retrospect, from the point of view of one who savors the memories of them.

This is to say that prayer, like marriage, is an act of faith. You know that it is good, that it is natural, and that it holds promise for you.

In the beginning, that is all you need to know. Specific expectations can lead to disappointment.

You might expect to become a stronger, more disciplined person, able to resist temptation and live a life of asceticism and purity. But if that is your intention in praying, you will probably find yourself becoming frustrated.

You might expect to gain more power with God, so that you can effectively heal the sick or work other miracles. Again, if that is your intention, you will be unhappy.

Prayer is not something we engage in because we wish to achieve anything. Prayer is communion with God. It is a matter of making connections with the One who stands at the center of all life and joy, and of learning to live with those connections all the time. That's all it is. Nothing more, nothing less.

Now, a great many things come of this, especially later on, when you have been at it for a while. But in the beginning that is all prayer is—simply being with God.

A great many people are frustrated with prayer because they don't understand this. They see it as some great romantic venture of the soul from which they return as conquering heroes, or as some equally marvelous merit badge contest in which they are given points for every moment they manage to spend in a posture of devotion.

But prayer is so much more simple than that and much more substantive.

Prayer is coming into the presence of the One who loves us all the time—more than our parents ever loved us even in the best of times—and waiting in that presence, merely *being there* in that presence.

That's all. Coming and waiting and being there.

Prayer, you see, is a fellowship, a meeting, a merging.

You don't even have to talk when you don't want to or don't know what to say. All you have to do is to become aware of the fellowship, to pay attention to it the way you would if you were with an ordinary friend.

Some people never learn to pray because they say they don't know what to say to God. Words are not easy for them. But you don't *have* to talk to God. God accepts you in silence as well as in words. All you have to do is feel God's love for you, and, when you feel it, respond in any way your heart wants.

It's really that simple.

Maybe you can see, then, why attitude is important.

You do not pray in order to get something from God that God was going to give you anyway. You pray in order to feel God's love and to give God your love.

What happens when you do this, of course, is that you begin to see how rich your life already is—how God has surrounded you with more gifts and joys than you were aware of.

But you don't pray in order to achieve something.

You pray in order to be with God.

THE BEST TIME FOR PRAYING

Saint Paul speaks of praying "without ceasing" (1 Thess. 5:17).

It is not as hard as it sounds, really. You merely learn to be aware of God's presence with you all the time, whatever you are doing.

A friend who commutes to work says that he sits and communes with God every time he stops at a traffic light. You can do it every time you open the refrigerator. Or when you brush your teeth.

The point is simply to turn your thoughts toward God at many specific times each day.

One way to do this is to practice remembering God when you are performing one specific action all week. When you are making up the bed, for instance. Or setting the table. Or checking your mail. Or walking to school. Then, for the next week, pick another action.

What you will discover is that you remember God when you are doing last week's action too. And the week's before that. It is a cumulative effect. Soon you will be thinking about God a great deal of the time.

But it is also helpful to have a *special* time each day when you concentrate on being with God. Nearly all the great saints—

those who have mirrored the presence of God in their faces and attitudes—have insisted on this.

It becomes the anchoring time, the one that stabilizes your entire day and centers it on God. Without it, your devotion remains diffuse and unfocused. Without it, you will not really grow in your knowledge of God.

Think of it this way. If there were someone you truly wished to get to know, to know in a very deep and meaningful way, you would not consider it enough to visit with that person only in the odd moments of your day. You would want to reserve a time when you could sit down with the person and be together uninterruptedly as you talked and listened to one another. The odd moments would be more valuable than ever in the light of this period of concentration.

It is the same in our relationship to God. We need regular time set aside for exploration and fellowship.

As for which is the best time of day for this greater effort at prayer, that is a matter you must decide for yourself after considering your daily patterns. People differ in their opinions of the best time for praying, just as they differ in their opinions of the best times for doing other things such as working, exercising, or reading the newspaper. A time that is good for one person may not necessarily be good for another.

What you must do is consider your schedule, reflect on it carefully, and decide when you could pray best. You might even need to experiment for a few days and see which time or times work better than others.

There are two important things to remember.

First, do not relegate your praying to a time of day when you are too exhausted or distracted to enjoy being in God's presence.

C. S. Lewis once said that "no one in his senses, if he has any power of ordering his own day, would reserve his chief prayers for bed-time—obviously the worst possible hour for any action which needs concentration."

It might be argued, of course, that if prayer is enjoying the experience of God's loving presence, there is no better time to pray than when one is weary and has exhausted his or her own resources. And in a sense that is correct.

But what kind of husband turns to his wife to give her attention only after he has completely exhausted himself through the affairs of the day and evening? Or what kind of parent reserves for loving a child only the moment when he or she sits half in a stupor at the end a long, hard day?

No, Lewis is right. Bedtime is not the best time for prayer—*unless* you find it to be a time of such inner relaxation and composure that you can concentrate better then on the presence of God than you can at any other available time. And some people *do* seem to be more alert in the evening than they are in the morning.

It is a matter which you must decide for yourself.

Second, once you choose the best time of day for prayer, observe it faithfully. This may be very hard for you, but there is a good reason for it: if you don't observe the time strictly, you will soon forget to observe any time of prayer at all.

Your intentions, of course, will be the best. You may be a busy person, and perhaps you feel it does not suit you to designate a particular hour every day for prayer. You may feel it more practical to be flexible and pray during a slack time during the day. And you will really mean to do that. But take it from the master of the flexible schedule: You won't!

You may be faithful to do it for several days, but then one day you will slip and fail to give your attention to prayer. A few days later you will slip again. And before you know it, you will have given up on it entirely.

Admit to yourself that it is very difficult to establish the habit of doing something new like praying at a certain time every day. It *is* difficult.

Then go ahead and do it.

In a few weeks it will seem as natural in the course of your day as eating a meal or brushing your teeth.

Then, when something interferes with your usual program of praying, you will miss it.

Richard Campbell Raines, a United Methodist bishop, made a habit of praying at the start of every day. If for any reason he failed to pray, he said his entire day was affected. A pall seemed to hang over his affairs, and nothing seemed to go right.

How long should this daily time of prayer be?

Again, that will depend on you, and on the method or methods of praying you find most useful. I once heard Bill Hinson, the late pastor of the First United Methodist Church of Houston, say that he could pray sufficiently in five or ten minutes. He said he was like the man who figured, "Why hang around the bank after your check's been cashed?" And there are others, like Martin Luther and Thomas Merton and Paul Tournier, who have said that even an hour passes in a hurry when you are in the presence of the Ruler of all that is.

If you combine your prayer with meditation on the scriptures, as some people do, you will require long enough both to study and to "listen" to the scripture passage. A time of simple meditation can obviously be shorter.

It is probably best not to be too ambitious at first, setting a longer time for yourself than you find comfortable and rewarding. Too long a time can cause you to become distracted or discouraged.

You might begin with five or ten minutes. That way you can tuck it into your present schedule without completely disrupting everything.

If you work at a business, you can even slip it into your lunch hour. Many Christian businesspersons make a practice of closing the office door at noon, sitting quietly at their desks in prayer for a quarter of an hour, then going off for their luncheon engagements. It is amazing, they say, how this affects the tone and content of table conversations.

If you are a stay-at-home mother or father, you can guard the few minutes between the time when the children leave for school, beds are made, and the dishes washed, and the time when you have to go to the grocery. If you are a high school student, you can fence off fifteen minutes during a regular study period at school, or at lunchtime, or when you first return home from school.

Make the period relatively short at first, and observe it regularly. Then, as the weeks and months go by, you will probably find that it has a tendency to grow longer. That is natural.

When you are first getting acquainted with a new friend, you are aware of a certain awkwardness. It takes a while to break through the strangeness barrier. Later, when you know each other very well, and find that you enjoy each other's company, the time seems to fly when you are together!

THE BEST PLACE FOR PRAYING

WHERE YOU DO your praying is not an all-important matter. Some people like to pray in churches; others, at their desks. Still others, like the late Frank Laubach, who had a tremendous prayer life, spend much of their time traveling, and so must learn to pray on buses, trains, and airplanes—not to mention in hotel rooms and restaurants.

But having a definite place is helpful in the beginning, just as having a specific time is.

It need not be a fancy place. Jesus told the disciples to go into a room and shut the door and pray there (Matt. 6:6). The kind of room he had in mind was small because none of the disciples were wealthy. Their rooms were probably very plain, with earthen walls and floor.

Perhaps the two most essential characteristics of a place for praying are, one, that it be quiet, so that you will not be distracted, and, two, that it be moderately comfortable.

Quietness is a must. True prayer, you will learn, is composed as much of silence as it is of speaking.

Some people are much more adept at "inner silence" than others—at discovering and maintaining an unflappable quietness at the centers of their being, regardless of what is going on around them. I once heard that poet Robinson Jeffers could sit for hours staring straight ahead, even when there were flies crawling on his face.

But even the best of us can be readily distracted from communion with God by the sudden ringing of a cell phone, the whir of a dishwasher, the buzzer on a clothes dryer, or noises from a television.

It may be, because of this, that you will have to consider the matters of time and place together when deciding where you can pray in order to have part of your house or apartment to yourself.

I have known several persons who made a practice of arising early in the morning, before their families were awake, in order to have a quiet time and place for their devotional lives.

As for the telephones, cell phones, iPads, and other devices, it would be good idea to turn them off for the period of your prayers. It isn't friends, family, or business associates you want to hear from during this time, but someone who is much more important.

The matter of moderate comfort is also important, especially in the beginning. This may sound strange if we think of Jesus' long periods of prayer in the wilderness, or the stories of holy persons who have sought refuge for meditation in the desert and the mountains. But that can come later, if you feel led to do it.

In the beginning, it is better not to be distracted by an unnecessary degree of discomfort. Let God *ask* for such signs of devotion, or decide that you will make a gift of them to God out of your growing love for the holy presence. Too much comfort, of course, is not good either. You don't want to be lulled into sleep by lying in a soft bed or sitting in a relaxing chair.

Most people find sitting at a desk or table quite suitable. Persons who work at home often like to sit at the kitchen table, so that they are praying right at the center of where much of their activity occurs. Or, if you prefer to kneel, the bedside or the edge of a rather firm sofa offers a modest prop so that you do not become physically tired or cramped while praying.

There is some reason for using the same place regularly for your prayers. Subconsciously, this creates an expectancy of prayer whenever you return to the place. Just as you expect to enjoy a meal when you sit down at the dining table, or to sleep when you go to bed, at your chosen place of prayer you expect to be in communion with God.

Some persons who have had great experience in prayer like to have a special place in the home that is used *only* for prayer. This, they say, heightens the sense of expectancy even more.

You can do this very simply, if you feel that it would be meaningful to you. Merely select the portion of a room you wish to use, or a large closet, or a small spare room, and arrange it with any simple furnishings that seem appropriate.

Some persons like to arrange an interest center, with such items as a Bible, a book of meditations, a candle, and a meaningful picture. I know several persons who use pictures or etchings of Christ. Roman Catholics often use pictures of Mary. I once decorated my prayer space with a bulletin board, on which I arranged a variety of pictures—usually postcards or magazine clippings showing nature scenes, children playing, the faces of the poor, and pictures of bread and other foods.

A few people I know use a *prie-dieu*, a specially made little kneeling bench with a shelf on top for a Bible, a prayer book, a hymnal, or other devotional aids. (The word *prie-dieu* is French and means literally "pray God.") Such an item of furniture fits unobtrusively into almost any room or office.

Some priests and ministers prefer to have their daily prayers before the altar or communion table of the church where the cup and paten represent the bread and wine of Holy Communion and remind them more forcibly of the presence of God in their lives. A few years ago, two ministers of the Church of England, the Dean of Liverpool Cathedral and his assistant, followed this practice, and spread the pages of the daily newspaper on the floor beneath them. As they prayed, they let their eyes fall on the newspapers to catch the names of persons for whom they wished to offer intercession.

In the home, you might like to pray with a bit of bread or wine before you as a kind of unofficial sacrament, to remind you of God's loving care for you in the wilderness of life. Or you might prefer bread and tea.

These matters are beginning to impinge upon the subject of one's *mood* in praying, and we shall shortly be discussing that.

But first we must give a brief consideration to the topic of posture.

YOUR POSTURE IN PRAYING

A GREAT DEAL has been said and written in recent years about "body language," and how we express ourselves non-verbally by the various postures of our bodies.

This is reason enough to be concerned about how we compose our bodies for prayer.

The position we assume while praying not only says something to God; it also sends secret messages to our own subconscious minds that either help or hinder us as we pray.

Actually, of course, prayer never completely depends on bodily attitudes. You can pray effectively while walking along the street, riding in an elevator, standing at a counter, or lying on your back. But as a general rule there can be no doubt that a humble, reverent pose is most conducive to the spirit of faithful devotion you are concerned to develop in your special prayer time.

Since ancient times, kneeling has in most cultures been considered the most respectful posture for approaching the deity. This was possibly a derivation from the practice of prostrating oneself before the king or queen or tribal authority, who in many cases held the power of life or death over the subject.

In the New Testament, we have the picture of Jesus praying in the Garden of Gethsemane on the night before his crucifixion, and, according to the description we are given, he "threw himself on the ground" in prayer (Mark 14:35). The Gospel of Matthew recounts the same.

This is the only record we have of Jesus' posture in prayer, however, and it is possible that the posture in this instance was dictated at least in part by the anguish of the crisis he was facing. Anyone who has sought the will of God in an agonizing life-decision knows what an appropriate posture it can be.

Common sense suggests that Jesus did not always pray in a similar position. During his days and nights in the wilderness, he probably prayed sitting down or while walking. We know that the Jewish people even in that day were accustomed to praying with their arms outstretched and hands upturned to God. We have no record, though, of Jesus ever kneeling to talk to his Father, or teaching that prayer should always be done on the knees. Jesus seems to have accepted for his disciples whatever mode they were accustomed to in their own background.

The disadvantage of kneeling to pray is that kneeling can become a tiresome posture when continued for very long. Some people, too, are afflicted by arthritis or other problems with their knees and cannot manage a kneeling position at all.

In some cases, therefore, it is probably better to cultivate the habit of praying in a seated position that will not tire the body or distract you from the important thing you are doing—namely, engaging in communion with God. The body can assume a quiet, reverential pose even when sedentary.

Or, if you wish to use a combination of postures, you can begin your prayers by kneeling, then rise and sit during the major portion of them, and finally kneel again as a final gesture of submission and commitment. You can even stand with arms outstretched and hands upturned, offering praise to God, then kneel or sit, and complete your prayer time by standing again in the original position.

Years ago, when I was younger and my body more limber, I prayed with a combination method and found it very rewarding. I would kneel until my forehead was against the floor, remain there a minute until I felt throughout my body the sense of my desire to pray, then rise and pray kneeling by my bedside. I would complete the praying by returning to the prone position once more. During this final moment I waited until I felt God summoning me to rise, and this always gave me a special sense of completion about my praying.

But again the whole point has to do with "inner devotion," with the posture assumed by the soul itself, and that is not entirely dependent on a regimented position of the body. You will want to discover the posture in which *you* are able to pray comfortably and meaningfully.

THE MOOD FOR PRAYING

THE MATTER OF MOOD in praying is a very intangible and difficult subject to treat, but we should at least consider it. In a sense, we have been talking about it all along, in discussing the place and time and posture of prayer, for each of these things is able to affect mood. But now we need to go further and say a word about your inner disposition in praying—how you compose your soul for what you are about to do.

If you go into prayer with the attitude of *Well, I hate to stop what I am doing and go to my devotions, but it is time and I must,* you will find it a lot harder to enter into the spirit of God's presence than if you think, *Oh, wonderful, it is time for me to sit down with God again and feel the renewing power of heavenly love.*

The person who is experienced in prayer often describes it as a time of genuine ecstasy, when tides of joy sweep over the exultant soul and the love of God seems to wrap around the one praying like a wave or cloud, triggering explosions of delight and adoration. This is the result of spending months and even years at one's prayers.

But it is easier to arrive at such a level of joy later if you can begin to feel it a little very early on as you go to your devotions. Do not dwell on the fact that prayer is a new enterprise for you, or that it is going a bit slowly (if it is), but concentrate instead on the more positive aspects of the experience.

Did you feel the presence of God with you the last time, even for a moment? Remember that as you go to your prayers this time.

Did you feel a sense of cleanliness and purity afterwards that clung to your mind for hours like the scent of a nice perfume? Then think about that as you go to pray now.

Have you begun to notice your environment more since beginning to pray regularly, and to feel more comfortable in it, as if it were truly God's world and you are truly at home in it? Let this be in your thoughts as you return to your prayers.

Prepare yourself for the joy of praying by *anticipating* the joy it will be. We do that in other things, don't we? If we are going out to dine in a good restaurant in the evening, we think about it all day long. If we are going to be with a special person for a while, we look forward to our time together, and even dream of what we shall talk about.

Why can't we do the same thing in prayer?

If thinking about the meal we shall eat enhances the dining experience, and dreaming about the person we shall be with prepares us for the excitement of being with that person, then why shouldn't we motivate ourselves for our encounter with God by anticipating the joy and meaning of the meeting?

Some persons actually go through a ritual of preparation before entering their times of prayer. Carlo Carretto, one of the Little Brothers of Charles de Foucauld, prepares for morning prayer in this way: arising very early, a long time before daybreak, he goes out into the cold night air of the desert and sits on a hillside, watching the stars. He looks at the various constellations and meditates on the grandeur of the One who created the heavens and the earth.

Then he comes back into the small hermitage which Pere de Foucauld built for himself, where the sanctuary lamp filled with olive oil flickers and casts its light on the earthen walls. Wrapping his bournous around him for warmth, he kneels on the sand before the altar and begins to pray.

Why doesn't he pray out on the hillside, under the stars?

Because, says Brother Carlo, he prefers to come to God before the Eucharist, where God has been presented to us as bread.

"It is here," he says, "that I have felt the presence of God most strongly; it is here that I have experienced for myself Christ's dramatic recapitulation of the history of salvation.

"And I always come back here when I want to make my way to the threshold of the invisible, because the Eucharist is the surest doorway opening on to it."

But the time under the stars is preparation. It stills the man's soul before he makes his approach.

"We need some moments of preparation," he says, "a little time in which to calm the soul, or to wake it up—a vestige of human prudence, so as not to turn up like brutes for such an exacting task as prayer."

It is in this respect, I think, that we ought to mention fasting.

Not many people today are acquainted with fasting as a religious discipline, but those who are find it to be a very effective way of preparing the self for engaging in serious prayer.

This need not mean total abstinence from food for a prolonged period. Actually, it can take many forms.

For example, you might decide to eat no meat on a certain day of the week, or to drink nothing but water all day. Or, if you are a lover of sweets and desserts, it could mean foregoing these for a period of time.

The idea is to willfully give up certain things you ordinarily enjoy—it is no sacrifice to forego what you do not like or would not ordinarily have anyway!—as a sign of your desire to follow Christ or to purify yourself for the service of God. In addition to benefitting your body, you are demonstrating your serious intention of living a sober, well-ordered life. And, while such signs are probably not very meaningful to other persons, they can be quite helpful to you in reaching new levels of relationship to God.

As a recent Lenten period approached, I decided that I would fast on each Friday of the season. Accordingly, I permitted myself only a half grapefruit at breakfast, another half at lunch, and a bowl of thin soup for dinner, plus, of course, a great deal of water. The first week or two, I became very weak and nervous during the day on Friday. But even then I sensed a new development in my prayer life, a feeling of being closer to God because I was making a conscious effort to purify myself for the approach of Easter. And, as the weeks went by, I experienced a renewal in my devotional life that was better than anything I had felt in years. It was as if my fasting were a gift I was giving to God, and my new excitement in prayer was a gift God was giving me in return.

But food is not the only deprivation we can exact of ourselves as preparation for prayer. We can also decide to abstain from looking crossly at others, or from speaking grumpily, or from making critical remarks. Some people find that these are more useful ways of honoring God than fasting. And even when they fail to live more positively each day, their time of confession when they first go to prayer becomes a meaningful basis for relationship to God.

Yet another form of preparation for prayer, practiced from time immemorial by Roman Catholics and increasingly used by thoughtful non-Catholics, is to make the sign of the cross on oneself as a confession of obedience to the Christian way. This is accomplished by placing the thumb against the first two fingers of the right hand and thoughtfully touching the forehead, the heart, the left side of the chest, and the right side of the chest.

I once heard a nun, who had been a Protestant and a home-maker until she was forty years old, say that she wished her Protestant friends were not so afraid of this simple gesture of relationship to Christ. Even if she were to leave the Roman Catholic church, she said, she would continue to make the sign of the cross before prayers, for she found the inward dimension of this symbolic action exceedingly helpful.

Many people, in recent years, have learned to practice relaxation techniques as a prelude to praying. There are many excellent books and CDs on these techniques.

For example, you may sit in a chair, get comfortable, and concentrate on relaxing your body.

Begin by tensing the muscles in your neck and face. Hold them in a posture of rigidity until you can actually feel the pain. Then suddenly release all the tension and feel the sense of ease rushing along the nerves.

Next, tense the muscles in your shoulders and arms. Make your fists tight. Hold this posture of tightness and discomfort. Then release the tension and sense the relaxation in these muscles.

Repeat the exercise with your stomach and lower back muscles, then with your legs and feet. Really draw your toes up until they feel cramped and uncomfortable. Again, release the tension and let the feeling of relaxation flow through your lower extremities with a sense of blessed relief.

When you have completed the exercises and feel peaceful within, adopt your position of prayer and begin to give thanks to God for the wonder of life and the miracle of your own body and how it reacts to the way it is treated.

The important thing, overall, is to discover some method of preparation which you find useful in your own spirit and personality. It may be the contemplation of nature, as in Brother Carlo's case, or spiritual fasting, or making the sign of the cross, or performing relaxation exercises.

Or it might be something entirely different, such as playing a hymn on the piano.

Or sipping a cup of tea.

Or engaging in actual physical exercise.

Or blanking your mind for a few minutes.

Or listening to music.

Or reciting a favorite poem.

Or taking a walk.

Or staring at a picture.

Or reviewing the events of the day.

The idea is to create a new mood in which to make your approach to prayer, to draw a line between where you were in the day's activities and where you are going to be when you submit yourself to God's presence. To enter such a new mood you may require nothing except the ready consciousness that you are about to enter into a time of prayer.

But the important thing is to enter the experience with anticipation and joy, as befits coming into the presence of the Most High and feeling the love and adventure awaiting you there.

THE METHODS OF PRAYING

F ROM THIS POINT ON, we shall be talking about the actual methods of prayer—ways of thinking or speaking or being before God.

Do not allow yourself to become baffled or discouraged by the number of methods. Most people employ only two or three methods during a given period of their lives, and it certainly is not requisite that you use or even remember all the methods. The fact that there are many methods is merely a reflection of the variety of human personality and the inventiveness of men and women through the ages who have sought new ways of understanding and participating in the art of prayer.

As in everything we have said, you will wish to seek the method or methods most suitable to your own personality at the present time.

One way of doing this is simply to try one method after another, allowing enough time to get the feel of one method before moving on. Then, when you have tried them all, you can decide on the one, two, or three methods you would like to use most constantly in your developing prayer life.

You may even invent methods of your own that you find more helpful and fitting for your pilgrimage in prayer, because prayer, after all, is a very personal experience.

And methods, when all is said and done, are only methods. They are a means to an end, not the end itself.

The end, in this case, is to be aware of living in the presence of God. It is to develop new ways of seeing and being in the world, so that we are more sensitive to *whose* the world is and *whose* we are, with the result that we live more fully, more happily, more exultantly.

And anything that helps to achieve this is a suitable method of praying.

THE PRAYER OF SILENCE

W E BEGIN WITH the easiest and yet the hardest of all prayers—the prayer of silence. Easiest because the brain is not taxed to think of words to speak to God. Hardest because most of us are so unused to silence, to waiting, to being still and feeling our souls become still.

Some of us have an absolute aversion to silence. We live in a world of sounds and noises—bleeping gadgets, ringing cell phones, chattering radios and televisions. If we are left alone for half an hour, we turn on a noise for companionship. We idolize quiet, rustic settings, but when we go there we take our cell phones and iPads with us.

Yet, from the beginning of time, and in all religions, God has been associated with eternal silence. Mystery is hushed. Holiness is awesome, still, unspeakable.

The greatest temples have always been those that embodied this stillness, not those that provided excellent acoustical qualities for the transmission of voices. By allowing us to leave the world of sound, they seem to usher us into the presence of the One who has been called "the wholly Other."

Perhaps the best way to begin praying, then, both when we are first learning to pray and long afterwards, is by coming before

God in quietness—by drawing near and waiting in silence, with no anxious straining after words or thoughts.

In the beginning, the silence may make us nervous.

Nothing seems to be happening.

No matter. Wait.

Prayer is not "useful" in the sense that certain other things are. We do not arrive at its benefits directly.

We are not dealing, after all, with a banker, an insurance agent, or a pharmacist.

We are waiting before the Creator of the World, the Most High God, the Transcendent One, the Alpha and Omega, the Beginning and the End, the Source of All Holiness.

God is so holy, in fact, that the ancient Jews would never speak the divine name. Only once a year did the high priest of Israel dare to enter the Holy of Holies and utter it. And even then, it is said, the people tied a rope around his ankle so they could draw him out if he should be struck dead while doing so.

Viewed in this light, what do we have to say to God? What *can* we say?

Instead, reverently enter the divine presence and kneel or sit without speaking.

Concentrate only on what you are doing—waiting in the presence.

Listen to the silence.

Will the presence speak?

Perhaps.

And if it doesn't?

Listen to the silence.

Without speaking, the presence surrounds you.

Your earthly ambitions are recognized as tawdry, your fears as groundless, your resentments as self-paralyzing, your hurrying as pointless.

Love, peace, joy, gratitude, the fruit of the spirit. These are the things that matter.

Bless the name of the Holy One.

This is what the silence comes to.

Move to other forms of prayer. Or, if you feel that the praying is over, return to your work.

But something is different. You don't feel so harried. Your very being is lighter, more spiritual. The Holy Spirit, the Spirit of Holiness, cradles your own.

Perhaps your heart will beat too fiercely when you try this prayer of silence, and you will wish to stop.

Try breathing deeply, and concentrating on that.

Inhale.

Exhale.

Wait before God.

Inhale.

Exhale.

Wait before God.

Feel the rhythm of it.

Many holy persons in our own tradition, as well as those from the Eastern religions, have employed this technique.

Next, let us consider a slight variation of silent prayer.

LISTENING TO GOD'S QUESTIONS

Some people have found this to be an effective method of waiting before God. Instead of concentrating on God and the silence, they tune themselves to listen for God's voice in their subconscious minds raising questions for them.

"Here I am, God," they say in effect. "I am trying to give you my attention. What questions do you wish to ask me today?"

Perhaps the inner voice will say, "Who do you love?"

"Why, I love you," the one praying will respond. And then he or she will think, *But I haven't shown it, have I? I have been too busy and self-indulgent. I have not honored the commandments.*

The answer is then modified. "I am sorry, dear God. I *want* to love you."

"Have you forgotten to write to your friend in the hospital?" the voice may ask.

"Oh, I did mean to do that, but it slipped my mind. Please, God, give her strength for this ordeal. Be very close to her now. Borrow from my strength and give it to her, God; she needs it much more than I."

"What about Joey? Don't you think something is bothering him?"

"I hadn't reflected on it, God, but I think you are right. He *has* been moody lately. Teenagers don't have it easy today. Please help him, dear God, whatever it is. And I'll be especially attentive to him when he comes home today."

More silence.

"Do you really love me?"

"O God, you know I do. Why do you keep asking me that?"

"Then why haven't you done something for that family over on Becker Street? The one whose father has Parkinson's disease?"

And on and on it goes.

You get the idea of how it might work for you.

It is an unusually hard and searching kind of prayer, and one that is especially helpful to the development of a thoroughly Christian conscience. Its benefits are often missed when we spend all our prayer time *talking* to God, instead of *listening*.

USING A SINGLE PHRASE

T HE ANONYMOUS CHRISTIAN mystic of the Middle Ages who wrote *The Cloud of Unknowing* advised using a single word as a prayer and saying it over and over.

"God" and "love" were two he or she suggested.

The idea is to use the word as a kind of mantra that induces a hypnotic effect in the soul. That way it constantly rec-enters the soul, banishing to the periphery of one's life greed, false ambition, anxieties, fears, and resentment.

"Thine only, thine only," were the words favored by the great Quaker mystic Thomas Kelly.

Kelly also liked to use a phrase from the Psalms, such as "So panteth my soul after thee, O God."

This variation of the method, concentrating on a few words from scripture, has always been popular in monastic orders. Since the early Middle Ages, monks and nuns have scoured the pages of the Bible, especially the Psalms and the New Testament, for simple, meaningful phrases which they would memorize and then repeat over and over as simple prayers of the heart.

Consider these parts of verses, and the effect of constantly repeating them in a prayerful attitude:

"The LORD sustains me" (Ps. 3:5).

"O LORD, our Sovereign, how majestic is your name" (Ps. 8:1).

"God is our refuge and strength" (Ps. 46:1).

"Let me hear joy and gladness" (Ps. 51:8).

"The LORD is your keeper" (Ps. 121:5).

"I will praise the LORD as long as I live" (Ps. 146:2).

"Blessed are the pure in heart" (Matt. 5:8).

"I will get up and go to my father" (Luke 15:18).

"I am the living bread" (John 6:51).

"In him we live and move and have our being" (Acts 17:28).

"All who are led by the Spirit of God are children of God" (Rom. 8:14).

"Come, Lord Jesus!" (Rev. 22:20).

You have but to turn through the pages of the Bible to see that such phrases almost literally leap out at you to be used.

Choose one and use it for a week. Then choose another the next week, and so on.

All of your life, whenever there is unusual pressure on you or you are facing some crisis or calamity, the phrases you have thus memorized and used as prayers will rise automatically into your consciousness and become holy food, nourishing your heart.

Do not be especially concerned about their theological meaning. Simply repeat them, over and over, until you do so almost unconsciously. At that point, they will begin to do most good, for then your spirit will be most yielded to God's Spirit.

Thomas Kelly said that is when God's Spirit takes over and begins to pray through ours, so that we are only blessed channels through which God talks to God:

> We pray, and yet it is not we who pray, but a Greater who prays in us. Something of our punctiform selfhood is weakened, but never lost. All we can say is, Prayer is taking place, and I am given to be in the orbit. In holy hush we bow in Eternity, and know the Divine Concern tenderly enwrapping us and all things within His persuading love. Here all human initiative has passed into acquiescence, and He works and prays and seeks His own through us, in exquisite, energizing life. Here the autonomy of the inner life becomes complete and we are joyfully *prayed through* by a Seeking Life that flows through us into the world of human beings.

THE JESUS PRAYER

Lord Jesus Christ, have mercy on me."

This is what is known as "the Jesus prayer." It is the English version of the Greek phrase *Kyrie eleison*, which has been embedded in the liturgies of the church since earliest times.

For centuries, it has been used in the repetitive manner we have been describing. The person praying it simply uses it over and over, like a chant.

Between the years 1851 and 1863, an unknown Russian Christian wrote a book called *The Way of a Pilgrim*, in which he described his experiences with this brief prayer. The book has become the classic statement of what can happen when one takes this kind of prayer seriously.

The Pilgrim met a kindly father of the church who shared with him the teachings of *The Philokalia*, which means "The Love of Good" or "The Love of Spiritual Beauty." It is a collection of the mystical ascetic writings of Eastern Orthodox fathers over a period of eleven centuries. The father whom the Pilgrim met read to him especially about the Jesus prayer.

"Sit down alone and in silence," read the father. "Lower your head, shut your eyes, breathe out gently and imagine yourself looking into your own heart. Carry your mind, i.e., your thoughts, from your head to your heart. As you breathe out, say 'Lord, Jesus Christ, have mercy on me.' Say it moving your lips gently, or simply say it in your mind. Try to put all other thoughts aside. Be calm, be patient, and repeat the process very frequently."

The Pilgrim found a job as a gardener, where he could live in a little hut and say his prayer over and over.

At first his praying went very well. Then it began to tire him. He felt lazy and bored.

He returned to the father for more instruction. Again the father read from the holy book.

"If after a few attempts you do not succeed in reaching the realm of your heart in the way you have been taught, do what I am about to say, and by God's help you will find what you seek. The faculty of pronouncing words lies in the throat. Reject all other thoughts (you can do this if you will) and allow that faculty to repeat only the following words constantly, 'Lord Jesus Christ, have mercy on me.' Compel yourself to do it always. If you succeed for a time, then without a doubt your heart also will open to prayer. We know it from experience."

The father gave the Pilgrim a rosary for counting his prayers, and told him to say the prayer three thousand times a day in the beginning.

At first the Pilgrim found this burdensome; but after a few days he came to enjoy it. When he would stop, he had a desire to keep saying the prayer.

He reported again to the father.

This time the father increased his assignment to six thousand times a day.

A week later, he increased it to twelve thousand times a day.

"And that is how I go about now," wrote the Pilgrim, "and ceaselessly repeat the Prayer of Jesus, which is more precious and sweet to me than anything in the world. At times I do as much as forty-three or forty-four miles a day, and do not feel that I am walking at all. I am aware only of the fact that I am saying my Prayer. When the bitter cold pierces me, I begin to say my Prayer more earnestly and I quickly get warm all over. When hunger begins to overcome me, I call more often on the Name of Jesus, and I forget my wish for food. When I fall ill and get rheumatism in my back and legs, I fix my thoughts on the Prayer and do not notice the pain. If anyone harms me I have only to think, 'How sweet is the Prayer of Jesus!' and the injury and the anger alike pass away and I forget it all."

It is possible, of course, to see a kind of neuroticism in the Pilgrim's obsession with the Jesus prayer, for he eventually came to care for nothing in the world but saying the prayer. As followers of Jesus, who went about teaching, preaching, and healing, we have much more to do in the world than continually to induce self-hypnosis through an incantation of Jesus' name.

But the Pilgrim's excess should in no way put us off the use of such a prayer; it is an ancient and honorable prayer, and one you will find rewarding. Try it for brief periods each day—say, ten or fifteen minutes—and see if this does not invoke a sense of Christ's presence in your life.

THE USE OF MERE SYLLABLES

THE PILGRIM'S USE of the Jesus Prayer bordered on the practice of nonverbal sound or mere unconnected syllables as a method of achieving a near-hypnotic trance, and suggests the possibility of using indiscriminate sounds or syllables for the same end.

This reminds us that many "authorities" who seek to instruct others in receiving the controversial gift of speaking in tongues advise the person praying to begin babbling various syllables until the Spirit takes over and leads in the speaking.

"Bub bub a loo la hum ta rah dum," the person might say.

Or "Jub a roo, jub a roo, da da cah ta too."

As the person relaxes and lets the syllables simply roll out, without any attempt to plan or control them, merely following wherever the impulse leads, he or she may enter a semi-ecstatic state in which the sounds seem to take over, as it were, producing utterance on their own with no conscious assistance from the speaker.

This, as I understand it, is what happens in most tongues-speaking.

Saint Paul acknowledged the legitimacy of such irrational speaking among early Christians, although he counseled that it should not be permitted to get out of hand in the congregations and become a substitute for clear teaching and sensible communication (see 1 Cor. 14:1-33). Perhaps it ought not to be too quickly dismissed as a form of private devotion, therefore, even though most of us are sociologically conditioned to regard tongues-speaking as a divisive, if not completely barbaric, expression of religious behavior.

Basically it is an attempt to break through the rational barriers that circumscribe the religious experience, allowing the subconscious part of the worshiper's being to join in the praising of God.

In Freudian terms, the id is released to dance and sing before God, where previously only the superego was permitted to speak. Long starved for the presence of the Holy by the forces of culture, including the organized church, it breaks forth with an emotional power that excites the person tremendously, for the person has probably felt nothing like it since the untrammeled days of childhood.

It is like a personal, private Pentecost!

We remember what Thomas Kelly said, "We pray, and yet it is not we who pray, but a Greater who prays in us"; and "The autonomy of the inner life becomes complete" when we are "joyfully *prayed through*, by a Seeking Life that flows through us."

Using the words of scripture or the Jesus prayer probably helps to imprint a religious "message" in the unconscious; but this complete release of the unconscious through impulses disconnected from words and meaning is probably very beneficial to some persons, especially those who have lived too strictly under the tyrannizing tendencies of their own wills and rationalities.

I have known persons whose whole lives were radically changed by submission to such prayer, because the praying opened them to the abundant joy of God's presence in *all* their activities, not only in prayer. They had *heard* that God is love—had heard it with their ears and minds. But in praying like this they *experienced* God as love in their total beings.

PRAYING WITH A MENTAL IMAGE

NEXT, I WILL mention the use of a consciously selected image as a focus for praying. This kind of prayer is also nonverbal in nature, and permits the participation of both the conscious mind and the unconscious aspects of personality. Instead of praying with words, you select an image or scene and project yourself into that.

You might think of yourself, for example, as a piece of wood bobbing along on the ever-moving waves of the ocean. God is the water under you, supporting and cradling you. With your eyes shut, you allow yourself to float among the waves, up and down, up and down, up and down.

If your imagination is especially keen, you can soon smell the clean, salt air and hear the screeching of the gulls overhead. Your body is totally relaxed, and your mind is simply drifting with the waves, letting God take care of everything.

This is an excellent technique for relaxing and can be used as a helpful prelude to other kinds of prayer. In itself, it is also a very meaningful way of letting yourself *feel* the goodness of God in your whole being and not only in your mind.

You can of course feel other aspects of God's relationship to you as well.

If your praying has led you to contrition for some sinful attitude or deed, you may wish to imagine the bit of wood tossed wildly about during a fierce sea storm. Thus you are able to experience God's love (for you do not sink!) and God's punishment at the same time.

The range of images for this kind of prayer is limited only by your own imagination or power to conceive them.

I have tried this way of praying in an art gallery, with astonishing effect. Standing before the image of a blazing sun on a desert landscape, I experienced the presence of God as a withering, constant blast of heat, purging my soul with dryness and desiccation. Then, imagining the same bright sun in an Arctic climate, I welcomed the presence as warmth and comfort against the freezing snow and ice.

Looking into the cool shadows of a great forest, I imagined myself walking there as in a cathedral of trees, a primeval sheltering, and felt the hush of all the earth, as though God hovered over it in awesome benediction.

Staring at a painting of a family gathered in a sixteenth-century country kitchen, I became entranced by the small black kitten playing under one the chairs. At once I imagined myself as the kitten in God's kitchen, enjoying the bowl of milk set down for me, playing among the chair legs and people's feet, and stretching languorously by the great fireplace where a kettle of soup was merrily boiling.

And so on, through dozens of pictures.

When I emerged from the gallery, I felt as if I had experienced a rare treat—witnessing both the artists' works and the presence of God in a unique fashion.

In Charles Kuralt's *A Life on the Road*, the late TV commentator describes a fantastic night he spent once in a cabin near Mount McKinley in Alaska. A bright light outside changed to a shade of purple, then pink, and suddenly seemed to shoot in a streak to the very dome of the sky. A priest in the cabin explained that it was the *aurora borealis*, the great Northern dawn.

"I had seen the northern lights before, glowing dimly on some northern horizon," says Kuralt. "This was different, a display of brilliant pastels that trembled over the silhouettes of the mountains, a big Wurlitzer jukebox in the sky. Ripples of color rose in layers from bottom to top and unexpectedly sent bright streamers flying so high that we had to draw close to the windows to see where they ended above our heads."

The priest, who lived in the area, went to bed. Kuralt and his cameraman could not leave the sight and sat watching until it faded away with the rising of the sun.

As I read this fabulous description, I could not help imaging myself at the cabin window with these men, watching God's handiwork through the entire arch of the sky. I saw Kuralt's silhouette against the windowpanes, and outside was the glory of the Everlasting God.

What a wonderful experience of prayer!

FANTASIZED IMAGES

A SLIGHT VARIATION of praying with images occurs when we make a less conscious effort to select an image and allow the image to emerge freely from the unconscious.

To do this, you must relax the mind and permit the image to float into your consciousness with the certainty that you will consider it as a prayer-image regardless of what it is.

You may be surprised.

With no threat of censorship, the image may speak of hate or violence or lust.

But let it alone if it does!

What you are after are the images from your unconscious—the things *it* bids you pray about.

Once you have got the image or images (you may wish to allow several to float up before you return to full consciousness and shut off the flow), you can pray about them. Lay them out one at a time before God and ask, "O God, what does this say about me? What is my subconscious mind trying to introduce into our conversation?" Then listen quietly, attentively, for the silent voice of God as it speaks to you about the image.

Another thing you can try is to let the image float into your consciousness, then allow it to do whatever it wants, to move in any direction it wishes, even to speak, if it shows an inclination.

Again you may be surprised!

I have a vivid memory of praying this way once while lying on the sofa as my wife prepared dinner.

First, the image of a fat, jolly little elephant floated up. It had exaggeratedly large ears and eyes, and looked very much like the cartoon character known as Dumbo, the Flying Elephant.

I "watched" the elephant walk happily along through the trees, feeling a strong identification with him. Somehow, I knew that *I* was the elephant.

He came to an opening in the trees and found a school carnival set up there, of precisely the type that was operated annually at my children's school.

Joyously, he trotted onto the giant Ferris wheel.

The wheel began going around.

Up and over it went, faster and faster.

Faster and faster and faster.

Suddenly the little elephant flew off through the air, backwards, and landed in the trees some distance away.

I was horrified until he landed in the trees, which led me to think his fall was thereby cushioned.

As my consciousness moved in closer to where he landed, however, I saw a crowd of people gathering around him, and I knew he was dead.

My little friend—I myself!—had been flung off the madly spinning wheel and killed.

"What does it mean?!" I asked in my prayer.

The answer was as plain as the image had been: I was going too fast and furiously on my own "spinning wheel," and if I did not slow down to a normal pace I was going to die.

That simple.

And I knew it was a valid message. I *was* going too fast at that time in my life. The wheel I was on was turning far too rapidly, and I was not taking enough time for God or family or the ordinary things of life. By praying about what I had been shown, and deliberately altering my patterns, I was able to avoid the sad consequences of the little elephant's mad ride.

One would not wish to use such psychological images as the *only* form of praying, but it can be helpful in prayer as an addition to more traditional methods. It is especially helpful in bringing the less conscious aspects of the self before God.

PRAYING SET PRAYERS

For centuries, many people have been helped in their private devotions by reading prayerfully the written prayers of others. That practice is still valuable.

Many books of such prayers are available, ranging from the Book of Common Prayer and other liturgical helps to the collections of private prayer by figures like John Baillie, Lee Phillips, Samuel Miller, William Barclay, Michel Quoist, and Marjorie Holmes.

The important thing is to find prayers that are sensitive and that evoke the spirit of your own personality as you read them. Then read them quietly, meditating on the lines as you do so, until they become your own offerings to God.

A good substitute for a prayer book, if you do not have one, is a hymnal. Years ago, most hymnals did not have music printed in them, only words. This is still true in Great Britain and Europe. People are thus encouraged to see that the poetry of almost every hymn is actually a prayer, and that the songs of the divine service provide a prayerful continuity to all our worship. Consider these great words from Isaac Watts:

O God, our help in ages past,
our hope for years to come,
our shelter from the stormy blast,
and our eternal home!

Before the hills in order stood,
or earth received her frame,
from everlasting, thou art God,
to endless years the same.

A thousand ages, in thy sight,
are like an evening gone,
short as the watch that ends the night,
before the rising sun.

Time, like an ever rolling stream,
bears all its sons away;
they fly, forgotten, as a dream
dies at the opening day.

O God, our help in ages past,
our hope for years to come;
be thou our guide while life shall last,
and our eternal home.

What a marvelous prayer that is! How it deepens our sense of the eternal Spirit and reminds our souls of their endless security in God.

And any decent hymnbook is full of such magnificent foci for meditation.

PRAYING THE LORD'S PRAYER

W E M U S T N ' T G O far from talking about praying set prayers without mentioning the greatest set prayer of all time, the model prayer Jesus gave to the disciples when they asked him to teach them to pray.

You remember it:

> Our Father who art in heaven,
> Hallowed be thy name.
> Thy kingdom come,
> Thy will be done,
> On earth as it is in heaven.
> Give us this day our daily bread;
> And forgive us our debts,
> As we also have forgiven our debtors;
> And lead us not into temptation,
> But deliver us from evil.
> [For thine is the kingdom
> and the power and the glory,
> for ever. Amen.]
>
> —Matthew 6:9-13

Surely this prayer has been prayed more than any other prayer in the history of the world. Every day millions of people say it in hundreds of languages. On Sundays, it is raised by thousands and thousands of worshiping congregations around the globe. For accurately reflecting the mind of Christ, it is the finest prayer ever composed.

Think of it:

It begins where all prayer ought to begin, by centering on God and God's transcendence. The mind and heart are thus composed for communion with the Holy.

The principal petition is for the consummation of God's reign in the world. Not for some selfish wish. Not for some fulfillment of the personal ego. But for the ultimate success of all God's intentions for creation and its inhabitants.

The only real prayer for the self is for daily bread—the humblest form of sustenance. There is no mention of meats or confitures or fancy desserts. Not even a mention of wine. Only bread, the most basic food of all.

And this prayer, as if by instinct seen to be too much, too presumptuous, is followed immediately by a request for forgiveness, for pardon. Why? Why should the one praying be pardoned? Because, in accordance with God's will, he or she has already forgiven all who have personally offended him or her. It is like saying, "See, God, I have done what you said, I have practiced forgiveness in my own life; now surely you can forgive me as well."

And finally, as if still recoiling from the idea of sin and evil, the one praying asks to be delivered from apostasy, from ever falling away from God in the world of evil and temptation. In a sense, this is an extension of the very first words of the prayer, where everything is centered on God. The one praying is horrified at the thought of ever forgetting the holiness of the deity.

The line "For thine is the kingdom and the power and the glory . . . " appears in only certain ancient manuscripts, and is thought by most scholars to have been added to the original prayer of Jesus by leaders in the early church who wished to adapt the prayer for liturgical usage. It does have a sort of climactic ring to it, and nicely underlines the earlier theme of the prayer.

If we never uttered another prayer in our lifetimes, but could repeat this one every day with complete sincerity and fervent intention, it would totally alter our existence. We would become stronger, happier, and inwardly richer than we ever imagined!

I realize there are some persons today who identify the use of the word *Father* for God as a patriarchal expression they would like to leave behind. Fine. Pray "Our Parent" or "Our Creator." The intent of the prayer will remain the same. But don't lose the benefit of this wonderful prayer over a problem with a single word in it. Besides, the Aramaic word in the text was *Abba*, the word that a small child calls his or her father, much akin to our "Dada" or "Daddy." Here, then, Jesus was providing a very intimate, warm, trusting way of addressing God.

If you want to deepen your experience of praying this prayer, I suggest that you read Mary Lou Redding's recent volume *The Lord's Prayer: Jesus Teaches Us How to Pray* (Upper Room Books), William Powell Tuck's *The Lord's Prayer Today* (Smyth & Helwys), or my own *The God Named Hallowed: The Lord's Prayer for Today* (Abingdon Press). Anything that adds to your understanding of the phrases of the prayer will enable you to pray it with greater joy and intensity.

It isn't any wonder that the earliest bishops and pastors of the Christian church devised the idea of assigning the saying of the Lord's Prayer fifty, one hundred, or five hundred times as penance for people's sins. If anything will burrow into our inner consciousness and change our attitudes toward God, the world, and our personal needs, it is this magnificent prayer.

MEDITATING ON THE SCRIPTURES

Meditating on scripture is surely one of the most ancient ways of entering into communion with God.

The very first psalm in the Book of Psalms pictures the devout person as one who delights in the law of the Eternal One—the law embodied in the first five books of the Bible, the Torah—and meditates on it day and night.

> Happy are those
>   who do not follow the advice of the wicked,
> or take the path that sinners tread,
>   or sit in seat of scoffers;
> but their delight is in the law of the Lord,
>   and on his law they meditate day and night.
> They are like trees
>   planted by streams of water,
> which yield their fruit in its season,
>   and their leaves do not wither.
> In all that they do, they prosper.
>
> —Psalm 1:1-3

The early Christians clearly spent much time poring over the Hebrew scriptures, letting God speak to their hearts about what had come to pass in their lives through the ministry of Jesus. Their preaching and teaching consisted primarily of references to God's promises in the scriptures, and of recounting how those promises had been fulfilled in the death and resurrection of the Messiah.

Throughout the centuries of the Middle Ages, as Thomas Merton has reminded us, the principal method of the devotional life, for any who could read, was *meditatio scripturarum*—meditation on the scriptures. Whole orders of monasticism grew up around the practice of *lectio divina*, or holy readings, in which the Bible was read for people to listen to what God was saying through the scriptures. For Luther and Calvin and Wesley and their followers, it was the same.

Whenever in any age there has been an outpouring of spiritual passion, it has been directly traceable to an interest in the scriptures and what God was saying to the world through them. We can scarcely expect a similar outpouring in our own time, or in our individual lives, apart from a similar interest.

The simplest way to meditate on the scriptures, of course, is to sit down in your quiet place with the Bible before you and begin to read in a book you have chosen—say, the Gospel of Mark or the Epistle to the Romans or the Book of Psalms.

Read thoughtfully, letting the ideas and images tumble freely and fully in your mind.

Read as though listening for the One behind all of it.

In the medieval monasteries, readings were almost always done aloud. You might wish to read aloud, too, hearing the passages with the ears as well as the heart.

If you have any difficulty in understanding what you are reading, or desire to be more enlightened about details of biblical times, you many wish to acquire a simple commentary to read along with the passages. Almost any Christian bookstore will be able to recommend such a commentary on the text you are studying. But don't become overly concerned about the parts you do not understand. Treat them the way Ben Franklin said he dealt with fish bones: he merely laid them beside the plate and continued enjoying the other parts.

It is important to read through a whole book, even though it takes several sittings, instead of skipping around and randomly addressing passages throughout the Bible. The writers had individual personalities, and the various books have specific settings and themes; these do not always emerge from short, random encounters.

You may wish to keep a notebook handy for jotting down insights and biblical phrases you do not want to forget. This way you can pray over them not only once, but many times.

It is a good practice each day to memorize one verse or part of a verse from the passage you have read and to use that as a prayer phrase in the manner suggested earlier. In this way you carry over your time of prayer and meditation into the activities of the rest of the day, and you insert the words deeply into your heart.

When you have completed the reading of the day's passage, stopping at a natural breaking point, rest silently in the thought of what you have read, so that you feel the presence of God breaking through into your life.

The God whose mighty acts are recorded in the Bible will assure you of the divine reality in your own affairs.

I recall an occasion when my life had dropped below the

spiritual poverty line. I had been quite busy for three months writing a very long book and had permitted my daily devotional life to wane severely. My wife and I were living abroad for the year, and I was very weary of dealing with the minor frustrations that can accompany the privilege of such a time, including the devaluation of U.S. currency abroad. To make matters worse, my father called to say that my mother was gravely ill and had been placed in the intensive care unit of the hospital.

Frustrated and helpless, I felt an impulse to reestablish my prayer life around readings from the Book of Acts.

I remember the day I did it. It was in early January, and I pulled my chair in front of the window where it would catch the warmth of the early afternoon sun.

I suppose I had read Acts a hundred times before, but it was as if I were reading it now for the first time. Every verse or two, I would stop and pray. I felt God's power and love filling my life.

How wonderful the Book of Acts is, I thought. *And how exciting to think that it tells such a small part of what was happening in the early church in those days. It is almost entirely confined to the stories of Peter and Paul—the first half of the book devoted to one and the second to the other. There is no mention of the Christian work in North Africa, where it was undoubtedly going on with vigor. No mention of the mission to India, where legend says Thomas went with the gospel, and where strong centers of Christian belief were later found. No mention of the work in Gaul, modern-day France, or in Spain, where the Roman culture is bound to have assured a ready entrance for the apostles of Christ. Antioch, the third-ranked city of the Roman Empire, where the followers were first called Christians in derision, receives a bare mention, no more. What a tremendous ferment the Spirit of God was causing in the world!*

I prayed for my mother with a new heart. It was as if I were right there in her room, four thousand miles away.

I felt God's power anew—in my life, in hers, in the world.

How silly we are to let a single day go by without reading the word of God and meditating on it!

FANTASIZING WITH THE SCRIPTURES

Several Bible teachers and group leaders in recent years have suggested using the stories and teachings of scripture as a basis for group exercises in meditation and reflection. I have tried this and find that it works equally well for groups and individuals.

The idea is this: First you read a passage of scripture.

Then, to meditate on it, you close your eyes and imagine that you are entering the scene you have read about or, if it is a passage of doctrine, that you are having a conversation with the author about what has been said. Give your imagination free rein for several minutes, so that a living drama takes place in your mind.

When the meditation is over, think about what happened in it, what was said, and how it all applies to your life now. Offer the insights to God and pray for faithfulness to incorporate them into your daily routines.

For example, suppose you read the story of the prodigal son in Luke 15:11-32.

Close your eyes and put yourself into the scene in the father's house when the son announces that he wants to leave home. You may want to put yourself into the place of the young man.

See the hurt in the father's eyes. Watch the slowness of his movements as he produces a money pouch filled with coins and gives it to the boy. Feel the pouch in your hands as you take it. *Surely*, you think, *I am now rich beyond all imagining.* The world looks bright and beautiful as you walk down the front path, as you stride off toward distant lands and your wonderful future.

Dream about your new surroundings—a large city with all the mystery and intrigue of Middle Eastern metropolitan areas, with crowds of people, noisy bazaars, herds of sheep and goats being driven to market. You are overwhelmed and excited by your surroundings.

Think about the parties you give, the way friends flock to you because of your generous nature and the food and drink you provide. They tell you that you are clever and attractive. You laugh and enjoy it all and think the fun will go on forever.

But one day a new reality dawns on you. Your money is gone. The friends don't treat you as well as they did. Creditors come banging on your door before you arise in the morning. You look in the cupboard and eat the last little piece of cheese. What will you do now?

Not to worry, you think. *I'll get a job.*

Like most Middle Easterners looking for work, you join the crowd of people standing at daybreak in the local square. The landowners looking for helpers will come there, select the ones they want, and give them work to do.

The first day, no one takes you.

Maybe the second day it is the same. You begin to worry. How will you eat?

Then, on the third day, a funny little man offers you a job on his farm tending pigs.

At least it is a job. You will soon have money to buy food.

But weeks later you find your condition little improved. The farmer gives you so little in wages that it is soon gone. Your situation looks graver and graver. Before long, you will be reduced to eating the bean pods you shovel into the pigpens every day.

One day you have a fever. You feel so tired and broken. You dream of home. You think of your father's servants and how happy and well fed they are. You wish you could be with them, that you could enjoy even a part of what they have. You think, *What if I went home?* You almost cry for joy just thinking about it.

That night, when the farm is quiet, you slip away from the little dried-mud hovel where you have been sleeping and start for home. You walk until dawn, when you stop by a public well and draw up some water. It tastes sweeter than anything you have ever tasted. The world looks clean and wonderful to you. You're going home!

Then imagine yourself in the scene when your father sees you coming toward your old home. You think your heart will burst. But you are also afraid. What if your father is angry with you? What if there is no longer a place for you on his land? You mustn't think of that. You must hope.

Your father pauses. He stares hard at you. He can hardly believe what his old eyes are seeing. You know you have changed, but he still recognizes you. He is running toward you. You have stopped in shock and exhaustion. Your heart is pounding wildly. He calls out your name. There are tears streaming down his face. He enfolds you in his arms. You feel his warmth and love holding you close. He is laughing and crying at the same time. So are you.

Home!

How wonderful it is to be home!

How excited you are!

You stumble through the little speech you have made up, but your father is too excited to notice. He brushes it aside as he brushes the years aside.

"You're home!" he says over and over.

The tears have not stopped flowing.

You get the idea. You may wish to stop at this point and pray about what you have been feeling. In what ways have you taken yourself away from home and spent God's gifts in wasteful ways? What were the circumstances that urged you to return to the Father's house? How do you feel about God's reception of you? Your praying will be deeply and richly informed by all of this. You will probably feel as giddy and lighthearted as the prodigal son himself.

Either now or in another time of meditation, you will wish to continue to fantasize about the story and imagine yourself in relation to the elder brother. What sort of person is he? What are his objections to the father's taking you back? Is he a very religious person? How do his views affect his religious behavior?

You may even wish to switch roles at this point and become the elder brother. Then you can discover in yourself your own attitudes of pride, selfishness, and resentment, and play them out in the exchange with the father.

If you do, you will surely have much to pray about afterwards, asking God's forgiveness for your behavior in the past and seeking guidance to be more loving and forgiving toward others in the future.

The scriptures are a vast repository of human dramas, and they offer us endless scripts for exploring our feelings, understandings, and commitments. Only a little imagination makes them come alive with power and efficacy for contemporary living. And this kind of fantasizing opens endless possibilities for prayer and meditation, so that God can communicate with us in ways we never even dreamed.

MEDITATING ON OTHER LITERATURE

W E A R E N O T C O N F I N E D to meditating on scripture, of course. There are many kinds of literature that offer insights and impressions well worth reflecting on and praying about.

Almost any bookstore offers a shelf full of books with devotional readings and meditation pieces.

There are several magazines that feature material to be used in this fashion. *Guideposts*, *Open Windows*, *Alive Now*, *Forward Day by Day*, *The Upper Room*, and *Weavings* are but a few of them.

And then there are secular books. Books of poetry can dazzle us with images that become springboards to prayer. The poems of Robert Frost. And T. S. Eliot. And Amy Lowell. And Gerard Manley Hopkins. And Donald Hall.

They may even prompt you to write little poems of your own, which can be prayerful offerings to God.

And there are the beautiful, sensitive writings of such persons as Annie Dillard, Frederick Buechner, May Sarton, Madeleine L'Engle, Mary C. Richards, Nikos Kazantzakis, James Herriot, and Elie Wiesel.

I literally prayed my way through Dillard's *Pilgrim at Tinker Creek* and Buechner's *Alphabet of Grace*. They are both profound and exquisitely written.

And Kazantzakis, with his Greek Orthodox ebullience, always makes me feel so much more alive to the resurrection of Christ and its effect on the world—especially in *Zorba the Greek*, which I try to read again every spring.

Some people, I know, are afraid of literature that is not specifically "Christian." That is most unfortunate.

No walls of orthodoxy or chains of tradition were able to bind our Lord. He went everywhere, touching the unclean as well as the clean, eating with sinners as well as Pharisees.

And, if the Gospels are any kind of record, he enjoyed the sinners more than the Pharisees.

GIVING THANKS FOR ALL THINGS

P RAISE THE LORD!" sang the psalmist. "O give thanks to the LORD, for he is good; for his steadfast love endures forever!" (Ps. 106:1).

Thanksgiving has always been one of the most delightful forms of prayer.

Do you remember the story of Jesus and the ten lepers? (Luke 17:11-19). The lepers came asking to be healed. Jesus told them to go and show themselves to the priests in the Temple. It was to be an act of faith on their part, for the law in Leviticus 13 and 14 provided that anyone who had been cleansed of leprosy must present himself to the priests for certification of cleanliness before being restored to society. On the way, they were all healed. In their excitement, they ran on their way to the Temple and their families.

All but one, that is.

One remembered, and came back to thank Jesus.

"Where are the others?" asked Jesus. "Were all of them too busy to return and praise God except this foreigner?" (AP).

Here is the point of the story. The one who came back was a foreigner. A "nonreligious" person. All the rest were too busy.

Jesus blessed the foreigner and sent him happily on his way.

We often miss that aspect—the blessing of thanksgiving.

If we do not take time to meditate on the countless gifts of God and offer prayers of thanksgiving for them, we lose many wonderful moments that would enrich our lives even more.

Sometimes, because we are not thankful, we become sorry for ourselves and feel neglected. It is in being thankful that we see how truly rich we are.

I have a friend who works with the deaf. Her work is very demanding and exhausting. Some days she begins to feel tired and depressed. But she is a woman of prayer.

"Whenever I begin to feel depressed," she told me, "I think of something for which I am happy, and I say, 'Thank you, Lord.' Then I think of something else for which I am happy. Again I say, 'Thank you, Lord.' Then I think of something else, and say it again.

"Before I know it, I've completely forgotten about being depressed, and my whole day is bright again!"

That is a wonderful testimony.

I was speaking at a conference in North Carolina and told of her experience. The next day at breakfast a woman came up to me.

"I have something to tell you," she said. "Do you remember sharing with us the story of the woman who gave thanks? Well, this morning about three o' clock my husband woke up with a terrible pain. He had gone swimming in a motel pool on our way to the conference and developed an inner ear infection. It got much worse during the night. When he woke up, the room was going round and round for him, and he was in agony.

"I didn't know what to do. I went out in the hall of our dormitory and knocked on a door. I told the man who came to the door that I needed help, and he got dressed and drove us to the emergency room at the hospital.

"An intern looked in my husband's ears but said he didn't know much about such problems. He gave him some medicine and told us to come back at seven, when another doctor would be there.

"The medicine didn't help. We came back to our room, and my husband was screaming with pain.

"Then we thought of your friend and her prayers of thanksgiving. We were on the bed. I was sitting on the edge and holding my husband's head in my arms, trying to comfort him. I thought of something in my life I was thankful for and gave thanks for it. My husband, despite his pain, did the same. I thought of something else. So did he.

"That was what we did until seven o'clock," she said. "We gave thanks for the blessings in our lives. I thought you would want to know how much it helped."

At seven they returned to the hospital, and the doctor gave the man an antibiotic and a sedative. He was resting comfortably when she came to the cafeteria to get some breakfast.

Try this method of prayer yourself. Not just when you're in distress, but as a daily method of prayer.

Most of us have no idea how rich we are.

Simply listen to the voice of the Spirit suggesting things for which you can give thanks. Then, each time, say a quiet thank-you. I think you will understand better than ever before the gift of God's loving care for you.

BLESSING YOUR MEMORIES

A SIMILAR WAY of praying is by blessing your memories.

You do this by recalling memories one by one, holding them before God for a few moments, and being thankful for them as you do.

Painful memories as well as pleasant ones can be blessed. Painful memories, too, are part of the fabric of your existence. They help to make you what you are today. And, if God accepts you as you are, then you can accept your memories as they are.

This method of prayer is a kind of therapy, for it is a positive way of dealing with parts of your past you have never been able fully to accept.

Let's suppose you are a man in your middle years. You are in your second marriage; your first wife left you after only two years of marriage. You have three teenaged children. You do not consider yourself a success in business, for you have changed careers twice and your monthly pay does not quite meet all the bills. Your father, with whom you never got along, died when you were married to your first wife. Your mother is a partial invalid living with your sister, and your sister complains about your not shouldering more of the load by keeping your mother part of the time. Your health is not as good as it was, and you are beginning to be troubled by frequent pains of arthritis. Your cholesterol level is high, and the doctor says you may have to begin taking medication for it if you cannot bring it down by diet.

How do you bless your memories?

Begin by recalling some *good* memories.

Perhaps the time you went fishing with your father, and he showed you how to bait your hook just right.

And the time the family went out in the station wagon and cut down your own Christmas tree on the farm of someone your father knew.

Lift these up to God with thanksgiving.

Then, as the memories come, don't exclude the bad ones, the ones that make you wince. Try to thank God for these memories, too, just as you did for the good ones.

For example, consider your memories of your first wife. She really hurt you when she walked off, didn't she? Hurt your pride. Left you alone. Life seemed to be over for a while there, didn't it?

You don't like to think about it, even now.

But do think about it.

Think how it was part of her growing up and part of yours.

Think how you would never have married your present wife if it hadn't happened as it did, or had the children you have.

You can forgive her now, can't you?

And thank God for that memory too.

Try this kind of praying sometime when you are in a reminiscent mood. It is an immensely rich form of prayer, for it brings to vivid presence the many experiences through which you have already lived.

It also has a theological validity.

The history of the faith of Israel, as we know it in the Bible, is primarily a *recounting* of the events in the life of the people, and a meditation on how God has been involved in those events.

When you sit prayerfully recalling the events in *your* life, both large and small, and then bless them by giving thanks to God for having lived the events and being able to remember them, you are engaging in the same kind of theological act.

It will deepen your faith by letting you see the panorama of years under the loving care of God. The result will be a greater steadiness in future times of crisis and pain.

This too shall pass, you will think, *and become part of the history of my life. It is good to live, and to give thanks to God!*

PRAYING ABOUT YOUR WORK

T HE AVERAGE YOUNG person or adult spends at least half of his or her time in some form of work or serious activity. It is only fitting that this should become the subject of our prayers.

Not in order to "succeed" in the world's eyes, or to make more money, but to be fulfilled. To be creative in our use of the talents and gifts God has given us. To be thoughtful of others in the way we do our work.

One of Jesus' most important parables was about three men entrusted with money to invest for their master (Matt. 25:14-30; Luke 19:12-27). Two were energetic, creative fellows and earned their master's hearty approval. The third was slothful and dull and was discharged by the master.

The parable was actually about the Pharisees, who were unimaginative stewards of God's grace.

But Jesus clearly had respect for careful, eager workmen; otherwise, the point of the parable would not have been so well made.

God is as concerned about our work as the other aspects of our lives, and this should encourage us to bring our work into the divine presence when we pray.

Prayer relates our subconscious lives to our conscious lives. Considering our work in prayer enables the Spirit to release hidden power and insight from the subconscious levels of our being, so that they may be used in doing our work.

If you are an athlete, prayer will help you tap the deeper levels of your prowess and energy as an athlete.

If you are a physicist, prayer will encourage you to take those intuitive leaps of the mind that are indispensable to scientific progress.

If you are an artist, prayer will help you to overcome the gap between the creative impulse and the artistic performance, so that currents of inspiration flow through your mind and hands with less resistance.

If you are a homemaker, prayer will bring you to a more thoughtful, resourceful attitude toward the sometimes repetitive tasks of your vocation, such cooking, cleaning, and grocery shopping, and help you to celebrate the presence of God in each action of your life.

Concentrate your prayer on what it is you have to do, either as an immediate job or as a lifelong vocation. Thank God for your work, which is actually one of the greatest blessings of your life. Then wait patiently in the silence and listen. Let the Spirit speak to your heart about new ways of approaching what you do; about how to make the best use of your energy; about what parts of your work may be unnecessary expenditures of your time and power.

Paul Tournier, the late Swiss physician, said that one of the most important aspects of his prayer life was asking God what opportunities he should *not* undertake. Praying in that way helped keep his schedule simple and manageable, and doubtless prolonged his life, for there were many calls upon his time.

David prayed about the temple he wanted to build for God, said Tournier, and God told him not to build it. If David had disregarded that and built the temple, it would have been a sin, even though David would have been doing it for God. In the same way today, God will tell us not to do certain things that in themselves may seem very praiseworthy.

God helps us to shape our work and our lives so they are fulfilled in the divine purpose.

Then, like Brother Lawrence, the famous lay brother of the Carmelites in the seventeenth century, we will feel that we are worshiping God as well when we are scrubbing the pots and pans as when we are worshiping at High Mass in the cathedral!

PRAYING ABOUT YOUR DREAMS

W E   H A V E   S P O K E N   often of prayer and the unconscious. Nowhere does the relationship grow stronger than when we learn to pray about our dreams.

Dreams have always had an enormous significance in biblical faith.

In the stories of Joseph and the pharaoh (Gen. 40-41).

Of Nebuchadnezzar and Daniel (Dan. 2-4).

Of Joseph and the angel of the Lord (Matt. 1:20-21).

Of the Magi and the warning not to return to Herod (Matt. 2:12).

Of Joseph and the warning to flee into Egypt (Matt. 2:13), and then to return to Israel (Matt. 2:19-20).

Of Pilate's wife, who "suffered much" over Jesus in a dream (Matt. 27:19).

Of innumerable "visions," many of which were probably dreams.

Many people through the ages have respected dreams as having not only reality, but *super*-reality. That is, they predict the future. They show things that are happening presently in other locales.

Whatever we believe about that, there can be no doubt in our minds today that dreams tell a great deal about the unconscious life of the person dreaming them. Psychological research has taught us much about this and is revealing more all the time.

When we sleep, the unconscious is freed from the repression mechanisms that are ordinarily at work in our minds. It is no longer subject to the rules of our daily realities and can run riot in the wild provinces of absurdity that are a part of our larger reality.

To a psychiatrist, dreams and parts of dreams that are remembered when we awaken are invaluable clues to our inner personality, to the part of us that is often beaten and abused and stuffed into a box by our conscious minds.

Research has shown that most of us have several dreams each night, even though we may think when we awaken that we have slept without any dreams at all.

It is possible to train yourself to be more conscious of your dreams, paradoxical as that may sound. Some persons actually set alarm clocks to wake them at various hours of the night, so they will be able to catch the dreams that occur at those times. Then they write down the content they can remember from those dreams and go back to sleep. Eventually they become more sensitive to the dreaming process and are able to awaken automatically when having a dream.

If you wish to record your dreams without turning on a light, keep a pad and pen by the bedside and scribble out in the darkness what you can remember of the dream. Then rewrite it in the morning while it is still relatively fresh and you can still interpret your nighttime scrawl.

What do our dreams mean? Since ancient times, men and women have tried to discover their significance.

"We have had dreams," said the pharaoh's officers to Joseph, "and there is no one to interpret them."

Joseph answered: "Do not interpretations belong to God?" (Gen. 40:8).

Do they not indeed? A psychiatrist may understand a great deal about our dreams. But the Spirit of God is supremely able to help us in the process of understanding our inner selves in terms of the images that come to us in our sleep and to put those images in the perspective of God's will for our lives.

The significance of this for prayer and the self is remarkable. Whenever we can come before God with a dream or part of a dream and say, "Here is what I have dreamed. How is it important to my life?" we have a greater chance of discovering what it is like to be whole in the coming rule of God.

Let me give an example.

Once, while living in Oxford, England, I had a dream in which I encountered a very unkempt young woman. Her hair was matted and unclean, and her slacks were extremely tattered. She followed me home. On the way, we passed a woman I knew who looked at the two of us very disdainfully.

My home in the dream, unlike any I had ever actually lived in, was unusually elegant and had very expensive furnishings. Inside it, the unkempt woman followed me around. Then, she startled me by saying something in German.

When I awoke from the dream, I realized that I had seen a woman of similar appearance in the city shopping area. She was looking somewhat longingly at the fruit and vegetable bins as if she wished she could afford what she was seeing. At first, I resisted offering her money for fear that it would offend her. But on another occasion, I approached her with the intention of pressing a few pounds on her. When I did, she bolted away like a frightened animal.

As I prayed about this dream, I knew it was at least partly about this poor woman, and I felt that God was saying I needed to make a more determined effort to offer her aid.

I also thought about the other woman in the dream, the one I had once known, who looked disapprovingly at the poor woman and me. I couldn't discern why she had appeared in the dream, but I prayed for her, asking God's blessings on her life wherever she was.

Why had the poor women spoken in German? As I pondered this, I recalled that I was soon to make a trip to Germany to speak to members of the U.S. Armed Forces. So I prayed for the results of that trip, asking God to bless those whom I would meet there.

What about the wealthy home in the dream? Even though I had never lived in such an elegant place, I realized how much finer my residences had always been than those of many people in the world. I prayed for them and asked for God to help me share what I had with others.

In this way, dreams can be thoroughly useful for helping us reflect on our lives before God because they come from the other side of consciousness. John Sanford, Morton Kelsey, and others who have written extensively about the Christian interpretation of dreams deal helpfully with the way interpreting our dreams can enable us to achieve deeper understanding of our selves. But, even apart from a sophisticated method of interpreting the exact meaning of the dreams, we can employ them to enrich our prayer lives and sense of devotion to God.

My own practice is to go to sleep praying, whether I am taking a nap or lying down for the night, and to awaken in the same manner. That way, I feel that I am entrusting the unconscious and its "messages" to God in such a way that the messages, however pleasant or unpleasant, become constructively related to my waking hours. Even a nightmare, which I am thankful to say I rarely have, can offer useful fodder for the ongoing life of prayer.

PRAYING FOR OTHERS

In the preceding chapter I mentioned praying for the disdainful woman who appeared in one of my dreams. I know several people deeply grounded in prayer who are very careful to pray for the persons who occur to them in dreams or other forms of random thought. They sometimes refer to thoughts about other persons as "impulses," and feel that there is often a good reason, even a supernatural one, that has led them to remember a particular person at a particular moment.

I think of a woman I know who seems to have uncanny powers of perception in this regard. Several times I have had a letter from her saying that she knew I was passing through some crisis of decision or time of illness and was praying for me. Each time she has been correct. She also writes to another friend in the same manner and has not erred in his case either.

This woman follows a very traditional and useful method of keeping a prayer list with the names of many persons on it. She reviews it each time she prays, interceding briefly for each person named on the list. But she also waits for God's Spirit over the list, so that the impulses she feels are often, I think, divinely given. Then, when she feels an impulse, she prays with real concentration for the person thus singled out.

The trouble with a prayer list, said C. S. Lewis, is that, given a few years, it can become so burdensomely *long*. Yet he could never bring himself to lop off any names from it. He would intend to; it seemed so absolutely necessary. But then, each time he would go to do it, he would say, "No, not today. Another time, perhaps."

We can understand his feeling. It is almost like deciding not to bring someone before God any more, without knowing whether or not the person will get there on his or her own!

It is probably best to make a *written* prayer list, though I have never done so. I try to keep a *mental* list, and sometimes I will be reminded of someone for whom I have forgotten to pray for a while and will feel very much ashamed of myself.

I often allow my mind to roam over the entire country, from east to west and north to south, remembering people I know in all the states, and then thinking of the ones I know in other parts of the world.

And of course intercessory prayer is as important for people we don't know as for the ones we do.

The world is so full of hunger and poverty and suffering of many varieties, including even the suffering of those who have too much of the world's goods instead of too little, that we cannot fail to cry out to God for it.

It is all right to pray for the poor or the hungry of whole nations *en bloc*, I suppose; there is hardly a way of avoiding it. But I also favor narrowing down the object of prayer as much as possible and beseeching God for such subgroups and individuals as all the women going through childbirth in Tanzania, all the children suffering with eye diseases in Guatemala, or all the wage earners with leprosy in Calcutta. I know this is a facile way of categorizing people, but somehow it seems a little more personal and manageable than even larger general prayers.

It is easy enough when you begin to pray for others (and sometimes even after years of such praying) to wonder what good it can possibly do the persons you are praying for.

This is not the place to deal with that problem. I recommend *"Pray for Me": The Power in Praying for Others* by Kenneth H. Carter Jr. (Upper Room Books) or my own *Bread for the Wilderness, Wine for the Journey: The Miracle of Prayer and Meditation* (Intermundia Press). Christians have always believed that it does make a difference when you pray for someone. Not just in you and your attitude, but in the possibilities for the other person.

Think of it this way: in a world where energy is the true basis for all life, prayer effects a transmission of your energy through the medium of God's Spirit to the person in need of that energy, regardless of how far away from you he or she may be.

It is not that you are trying to countermand God's will for the person. Indeed, you pray *within* God's will and ask that it be done. But you are lending your willful energy to God for that person's use if God wills that the person have it.

Beyond that, you need not question. Your part is merely to lend your love and energy. And if you have been faithful in your devotional life, so that your faith in God is firmly grounded, you will then be able to accept with gratitude whatever God wills for the person.

Some persons pray for others by merely thinking or mentioning aloud their names. Others say they like instead to concentrate on the faces of those they are praying for, getting a mental picture and simply holding it for a little while in the presence of God. I personally favor doing both.

First, I wait quietly, thinking about the person until I get a clear image.

I try to listen to the Spirit, to see if I can hear what it is the person really needs. Sometimes it is not what my first impression suggested that the person needed.

Then I make an actual petition for the person, always concluding with something like the phrase, "Your will be done," for it would be most arrogant to assume that I was invariably right about what he or she requires.

Having used the word *energy* as a metaphor for what happens in intercessory prayer, I should say a brief word here about prayers for the dead.

Roman Catholics have always believed that it is a duty to continue to pray for the souls of those who have died. They also believe that those who have died can continue to pray for us.

Although the Bible does not make much of this idea, it does speak of baptism for the dead (1 Cor. 15:29), and seems to support praying for them in at least a couple of ways. One is in Jesus' story of the rich man and Lazarus (Luke 16:19-31), in which the rich man who has died and is in torment carries on a dialogue with God, first about his own suffering and then about warning his brothers who have not yet died. Another is the imagery throughout the Book of Revelation, which seems to suggest a kind of universal complicity in prayer and yearning that involves both the saints still living on earth and those living in heaven.

I think it is a good idea for us to accept the notion much as the New Testament does, without either setting it at the center of our belief and concerns or dismissing it entirely. When we feel the inclination, we may remember in prayer those who have died and take comfort in believing that they also pray for us.

On this point, I rather like what C. S. Lewis said to his friend Malcolm Muggeridge: "At our age the majority of those we love best are dead. What sort of intercourse with God could I have if what I love best were unmentionable to Him?"

Again, I believe the word *energy* may be the key.

The first law of energy is that it can be neither created nor destroyed. It can only be moved around.

What becomes of the energy of the soul of one who dies? I believe it still exists for us—if indeed it was ever *for* us before death. And I see little reason that the transference of energy through prayer that occurred during life should stop because a person's body has died.

But I do not wish to persuade you of something that is against the grain of your natural inclination for belief. It is a matter you must decide for yourself. And there are certainly enough persons for you to worry about among the living without burdening yourself too much with the dead!

The important thing is for you to learn in prayer to make your own energies available to God on behalf of other persons who need them. Intercessory prayer is indispensable, regardless of what other kind of prayer we normally prefer.

In no other way, I think, do we realize quite so perfectly the meaning of the phrase "the communion of the saints."

FANTASIZED SCENES

THIS KIND OF PRAYER is closely related to praying about one's dreams, because it involves praying about daydreams.

It is especially useful, when I am tired, depressed, or confused, and other kinds of praying seem to require more of me than I feel like giving. This method of prayer can be utterly refreshing.

The idea is to get very relaxed, imagine a scene, then let yourself "enter" the scene and wander about in it, doing whatever your unfettered self wishes to do. Afterward, you reflect on what happened in the fantasy and offer yourself in prayer to God.

Relaxation really is the key to this method. You should feel relaxed in your hands and feet, your arms and thighs, your neck and back, your chest.

Once you have gotten the knots out of your system and are sitting comfortably in a chair or lying comfortably on the floor or on a bed, let yourself go.

Imagine a meadow scene.

Or a seashore.

Or a lonely mountainside in the sunset.

Walk into the picture. Literally put yourself there.

Enjoy it; don't hurry.

Maybe you see someone coming toward you.

Who is it?

What happens when you meet?

Perhaps you go further, either alone or with the other person.

You get the idea. It is a wandering of the heart and mind, an excursion of the inner spirit.

Then, when it is over and you have "come back" to yourself, to the present realities of the room where you are, meditate on the memory of what took place. Talk to God about it.

Try it. You may be surprised at what you learn, and how good it feels.

This method of praying was first developed in the sixteenth century by Saint Ignatius, the founder of the Jesuits, who used it in his *Spiritual Exercises* to draw his followers closer to Christ. I learned it first not from reading Saint Ignatius, but from my friend Wayne Pipkin, a college and seminary professor.

Wayne tells about an experience he had with it during a very tense time in his life. He had moved, not long before, from the university where he was a church history professor to a new role as the director in a seminary system. Now the seminary was considering the possibility of closing, and it would mean that he would have no job.

Wayne worried about how he would take care of his wife and two young daughters. Perhaps they would have to sell their home and move in with one set of parents until things improved. In the midst of this anxiety, Wayne tried this method of meditative prayer.

He imagined that he was standing on a sandy bluff overlooking the ocean. It was a beautiful, clear day, and he could feel the spray from the salt air and smell the tangy odor of the sea. Seagulls were flying overhead.

He descended from the bluff and walked along the rocky shore, feeling very relaxed and at peace with the world. As he walked, he saw a bottle floating in the waves. It appeared to have a message inside.

He watched as the bottle bobbed in the waves, constantly disappearing and reappearing, gradually washing in to shore.

Suddenly he realized that the message must be for him. Eagerly, he ran forward into the water to rescue it. Surely it was the answer to his problems!

He caught the bottle and opened it. He removed the message, and found that it was in Latin.

"*Hodie Christus natus est*," it said. "Today, Christ is born."

Wayne was disappointed. What did that particular message have to do with his situation? God had let him down.

But as Wayne meditated on the message, he began to see how important it was to him. It was what he had forgotten.

"Today, Christ is born."

In his anxiety, he had lost the center of his faith. Now, here was a message to remind him of the center. As he thought and prayed about it, the fact of Christ's birth and life and death and resurrection found its way back to the heart of Wayne's life, displacing all his worries.

"I had become so obsessed with the future," he said, "that I had forgotten the central affirmation which gave meaning and hope for the present. When the words appeared to me on the page in the context of that meditation, it was not an idle affirmation of faith. Rather, it was a rekindling of faith down at the very roots of my being. In the midst of apparent insecurity, I discovered an insight into lasting security."

I experienced something similar when practicing this method of prayer. It was in the month of March, and I was extremely tired. I had spent all of January wrestling with a vocational decision. Then in February my wife's mother had an operation and died, and we made several trips home. My Lenten speaking schedule had gotten out of hand, and I seemed to be running off in all directions when I was not in class with my students. My emotional tension seemed to be about a hundred percent higher than I could stand, and going higher all the time.

On that day I took an afternoon nap. As I was awakening into semiconsciousness, I began a fantasy meditation.

I imagined that I was walking out the curving driveway to my mailbox. It was a warm, beautiful spring day, and the birds were singing happily all around. Flowers were blooming in great profusion—daffodils, tulips, and crocuses. The dogwood trees were blooming too.

When I reached the mailbox and opened it, there was a letter inside. I knew it was the message I needed, just as Wayne had known when he saw the bottle in the ocean. I could hardly wait to open it!

My fingers fumbled at it nervously. At last I had the message out. It said, "God is love."

That was all.

"God is love."

Like Wayne, I was at first disappointed. *I knew that*, I thought.

But as I meditated on it, I realized that this message was precisely what I needed to hear.

Down beneath it all—the vocational struggle, the death of a loved one, the physical exhaustion and tension—was the unshakable love of God.

Tears filled my eyes as I lay there on the bed, and I gulped, "Thank you."

I felt completely refreshed when I got up. It was just what I needed!

Try it yourself sometime. It may be what you need too.

AN IMAGINARY CONVERSATION WITH CHRIST

W ALTER SAVAGE LANDOR, a nineteenth-century liter-
ary figure, wrote a famous series of *Imaginary Conversations* that
depicted great persons of history talking with each other. Some
of the insights provoked by these conversations are amazing.
Suppose you were to carry on a similar conversation with Christ.
What do you think it might reveal?

The secret of such a conversation is to write it in the form of
a dramatic dialogue, and to do so without pausing to think while
writing. That is, the flow of dialogue should be as spontaneous as
possible, with the unconscious side of your being supplying most
of the words.

Here is how a sample dialogue might look:

ME: Lord, I am feeling totally self-satisfied these days. Does
that mean I have been out of touch with you?

CHRIST: Maybe you have been out of touch with those
who are suffering.

ME: You mean the poor? I know I am well off.

CHRIST: There are many children who are starving—in Asia, in Africa, in Latin America.

ME: But they are so far away. What can I do about them?

CHRIST: What have you tried to do?

ME: Well, . . . nothing, I suppose. I do give at church.

CHRIST: What do you give, a few dollars? What is that compared to their suffering? If they were your children, you would do anything to save them. *Anything*.

I confess that this is one of my own imaginary dialogues. It was a scathing one and led to my making a greater effort to serve Christ through the hungry of the world.

Not all dialogues are as self-indicting as this. Often they are strengthening or comforting. And sometimes they are filled with love and peace and the simple joy of relationship.

The words in such conversations can hardly be taken as the real words of Jesus to us. But it is entirely possible that the Spirit of Christ does release understandings from deep within us that convey striking insights we could not attain by ourselves.

The important thing, once we have discovered the insights, is to focus on them in prayer and meditation until we feel our lives submitting to God's presence. Then we know that the imaginary dialogue has led to real togetherness with God's Spirit!

SUBCONSCIOUS WRITING

THIS METHOD OF praying or finding insights for prayer is similar to the imaginary conversation method. Only, instead of writing a dialogue, you write simple statements as they occur to you.

Again, the important thing is not to edit anything, but to let the writing simply flow out of your inner self. Don't think of a particular sentence, "Oh, how silly! I mustn't put that down." In fact, don't think at all while you are writing. Merely get a starting sentence and begin writing. Let the words tumble out without being conscious of them.

You may wish to focus your writing around a particular problem you are having or an idea that has been haunting you. You can do this by having the idea or problem in mind as you write the first sentence. But don't exercise any more control than this. Let your subconscious mind take over.

Suppose, for example, that you are concerned about a vocational opportunity that has come your way and wish to get some of your unconscious feelings out in the open to be considered in prayer. Your subconscious writing might read like this:

I am really concerned about that job. It has great appeal for me. I like the people I would be working with. I am not valued where I am. It is terrible to work where you don't feel wanted. My parents never acted as if they wanted me. I wonder if I act as if I don't want my children. I would hate to die now, without showing them more love. If I take that job and feel more love in it, maybe I will show more love. Does God love me? I am unlovable sometimes. Maybe I would feel that way anywhere. Perhaps people love me where I am, and I cannot feel it. I must sort this out.

This is an actual paragraph written by a woman in early midlife. It was her first experience with subconscious writing. She was greatly surprised, examining it later, to see how much it revealed about her. She saw that her real problem was less with her present job than with her feelings of unworthiness. These feelings, she realized, caused her to withdraw from others. This, in turn, made her feel neglected and disliked.

As the woman focused on this insight in prayer, she came to feel more self-worth through God's acceptance of her and decided to stay in the job where she was. She developed two goals for her life. One was to learn to interact more healthily with her colleagues at work, and the other was to show more affection toward her children.

You may find, if you like to write down your feelings, that this is a meaningful way to know your inner self better.

Begin by writing as I have suggested. Do not think about what you are writing. Concentrate instead on the *flow*. Review what you have written, noticing any thoughts that particularly strike you. Then meditate and pray about these, asking God to reveal to you new understandings or new directions for your life.

And be prepared for some changes!

KEEPING A PRAYER JOURNAL

Have you ever kept a diary?

A prayer journal is a kind of diary with one difference: all you enter in it are remarks about your prayer life.

The experiences you have.

The thoughts that come to you while you're praying.

How your prayer life is affecting the rest of your life.

What you're having trouble with in your praying.

What God seems to be asking of you as you pray.

It needn't be terribly formal. In fact, the more casual the better. You can abbreviate words if you like, and the handwriting is not very important.

What is important is to keep a spiritual record of the time you are spending in prayer. And then to review the record from time to time.

You will find that this prompts new reflections. You may begin praying about things you wouldn't otherwise have considered.

It isn't easy to discipline yourself to do it, unless you naturally enjoy writing. In fact, it is probably harder than the discipline of prayer itself. But it is very rewarding.

John Wesley kept a prayer diary that fills several volumes.

One Methodist minister friend wrote this when we was having trouble keeping up with his entries:

> Well, my hat's off to ole John Wesley. How he ever covered 225,000 miles, mostly on horseback, preached 44,400 sermons, carried on extensive correspondence, oversaw the fledgling Methodist Church, and still found time for daily entries in his journal I'LL NEVER KNOW!

But the journal was a measure of Wesley's spirit—or the Spirit that was in his spirit. Over and over again on the same day, Wesley talks about praying. Preached at one little town and prayed as he rode to the next. Had tea with a poor family and prayed. Went to lunch with a local minister and prayed. Preached and prayed as he rode on. Had tea again and prayed. Wrote letter and prayed. Preached in the late afternoon and prayed as he rode to a hotel. Had dinner and prayed.

The man was a praying fool. Or a genius of a Christian.

I'll never forget the sense of awe that fell over me as I stood one day in the prayer room of his home in London. His prayer bench was situated near the window looking out on Wesley's Chapel. A Bible and a prayer book lay atop the bench.

I remember thinking, *The world has changed from that kneeling bench.*

The secret of a journal is the delight you take in making a record of what you have felt and experienced. You might put in something like this:

> Had the strangest impression as I was praying today that elderly Mrs. Arden was in some kind of unusual need. Prayed for her, asking God to supply whatever it was. Later, after lunch, decided to walk down and look in on her. She has

had the flu since the day before yesterday, and no one there to look after her. Prepared some soup and sat with her as she ate it. Told her about the prayer. "My mother was right," she said. "How is that?" I asked. "More things are wrought by prayer than this world dreams of," she said.

Or, on a bad day, perhaps something like this:

Had trouble praying today. Felt depressed and lonely. Judy was leaving for six weeks, and I knew the house would feel empty. My back ached when I had been kneeling only a few minutes, and I was afraid I was going to have another pinched nerve. I guess some days are like that, God. I'm sorry.

Always be honest about your feelings and emotions. Don't let the desire to sound good lure you into writing things that aren't so. That would negate the whole purpose of the journal, which is to give you perspectives on yourself and your prayer life.

Don't worry if there are more negative entries than positive. Or if most of them sound rather dull.

Your eye will always fall on the one that doesn't, and you will be thankful you wrote it down so it wouldn't be forgotten.

You will learn even from your more critical entries. Like this one, adapted from a friend's journal:

Thomas Merton speaks of the "desert place" as the abode of contemplative prayer. But how can God come in silence if I am not silent? How can God fill my empty place when I have not emptied it? How can love surround me when I run from it? "Be still, and know that I am God." Lord, help me to make a silence in the desert place of my soul.

But occasionally you will thrill to see that you have written something like this:

Cannot begin to describe the mingled sense of awe and ecstasy I felt while praying today. Very unusual. Had been reading Paul's letter to the Ephesians, chapter three, and meditating on each verse and phrase. When I came to verse eight, which says, "Although I am the very least of all the saints, this grace was given to me," I felt very strange and light-headed. I kept repeating the verse. Maybe seven or eight times. "To *me*," it says. "To *me*." It was as if I were in the presence of God and all the angels, and Mozart was playing everywhere, or the *Hallelujah Chorus*, and I had no sense of time passing or anything! It was wonderful!

It is important to make an entry every day, just as you pray every day. And don't worry about its being a fancy notebook. An inexpensive one will do very well. It is what you put in it that will make it valuable!

CONCLUSION

T HERE IT IS. A little introduction to the techniques of praying. I
hope you will find it useful but do not take it overly seriously.

Techniques are only techniques. They are a means to an end.
It is the presence of God you are really after.

"Mettez-vous en la présence de Dieu," Saint Francis de Sales
invariably began his meditations. "Put yourself in the presence of
God." *That* is what you are after. The rest is straw.

If any of the things mentioned in this book are useful as a
means to an end, I am glad.

If not, please do not stop looking. Prayer *is* real. It is worth
learning. Don't let anything written in this little book put you off
the track.

In looking back over the book, I am struck by one thing. That
is, how many of the techniques have to do with the unconscious
mind.

Obviously, there is much more to us than our egos, our conscious minds, our rational beings. We are dreams, emotions, fears,
anxieties, hopes, loves, hates—all kinds of non-compressible,
non-analytical things.

And if we are to belong to Christ, then we must belong to
him entirely, below the level of consciousness as well as above it.

Therefore prayer must spill into all of life, and all of life must get into our prayers.

There must be no holding back.

Everything belongs.

Our nervousness.

Our aggression.

Our sexuality.

Everything.

God can handle it. We needn't fear to be honest before the Eternal One.

It is *ourselves* we are afraid of, don't trust, endeavor to deceive. That would be laughable if it weren't so true. If we can just get through that barrier—the barrier of the self—life will be what it was meant to be.

God is waiting. And it is *prayer* that will get us through. Don't give up until you've made it!

I said in the beginning of this book that *time* and *place* are important in the discipline of prayer. They are, in terms of anchoring ourselves in the discipline.

But I am sure you have already grasped a significant truth: Once you have established your discipline, your regular time of communing with God, prayer will begin to spill out of the time and place you have chosen into all the other times and places of your life.

Using the variety of methods we have discussed, you will find yourself praying the Jesus prayer, fantasizing with images, blessing your memories, praying about your dreams, and focusing on the presence of God in other ways.

And, by the same token, you will be shifting into these many kinds of prayer in all the different places where you find yourself—

at work, at school, at the grocery store, walking through a shopping mall, driving on the freeway, eating a meal, strolling in the park, sitting in front of the TV, or lying in your bed.

The wonderful secret of prayer is that once you experience a breakthrough and begin to sense the joy and excitement of living in the presence of God, you can't get enough of it. It becomes a way of life. It moves into every area of your existence. In one way or another, you find yourself, as the apostle Paul put it, praying "without ceasing."

One of my students in a prayer seminar became so excited about this that he turned through the remainder of his prayer journal and wrote the word GOD in big letters on every page.

That is how you will feel, and it is the greatest feeling in the world.

ABOUT THE AUTHOR

John Killinger has served as minister of the First Presbyterian Church of Lynchburg, Virginia, the First Congregational Church of Los Angeles, and Marble Collegiate Church in New York City. He taught at Vanderbilt Divinity School, Princeton Theological Seminary, the University of Chicago Divinity School, and was Distinguished Professor of Religion and Culture at Samford University. A prolific writer, he is the author of seventy books, on subjects ranging from prayer and spirituality to theology and modern literature. Among his more recent writings are *Hidden Mark, The Zacchaeus Solution,* and *Stories That Have Shaped My Life and Ministry.* After serving as pastor of the Little Stone Church on Mackinac Island, Michigan, for eight years, he retired with his wife Anne to Warrenton, Virginia.

He still travels throughout the country to speak for churches and church assemblies, hold workshops for ministers, and lead retreats on prayer and spirituality.